BRITISH RAILWAYS

PAST and PRESENT

No 34

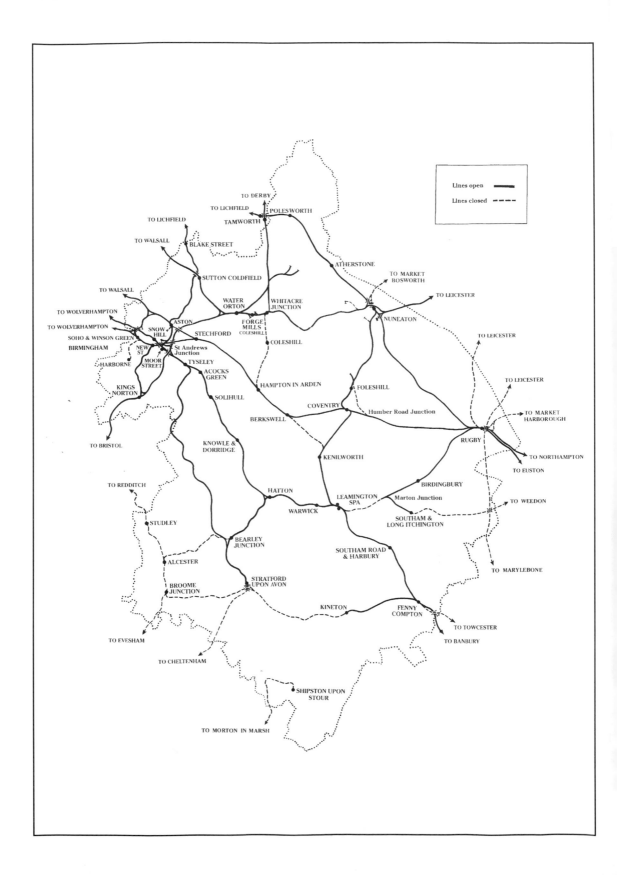

BRITISH RAILWAYS

PAST and PRESENT

No 34

Warwickshire

Roger Siviter ARPS

Past and Present

Past & Present Publishing Ltd

First published in 2001

British Library Cataloguing in Publication Data

A catalogue record for this book is available from the British Library.

ISBN 1 85895 160 7

Past & Present Publishing Ltd
The Trundle
Ringstead Road
Great Addington
Kettering
Northants
NN14 4BW

Tel/Fax: 01536 330588
email: sales@nostalgiacollection.com

Maps drawn by Christina Siviter

Printed and bound in Great Britain

ACKNOWLEDGEMENTS

I should like to thank the following people for all their help in compiling this book: the staff at Past & Present Publishing Ltd; all the railwaymen who made it all possible; my wife Christina for the maps and the typing; Michael Mensing and all the other photographers credited herein; and last, but not least, the many people who allowed me access to their land in order to obtain those elusive 'present' pictures.

BIBLIOGRAPHY

Warwickshire Railways *by Mike Hitches (Sutton Publishing)*

A Regional History of the Railways of Great Britain: Volume 7, The West Midlands *by Rex Christiansen (David & Charles)*

Rails Across The City *by John Boynton (Mid England Books)*

British Railways Past & Present: No 5, The West Midlands *by John Whitehouse and Geoff Dowling (Past & Present Publishing)*

British Railways Past & Present Special: Snow Hill to Cheltenham *by Roger Siviter (Past & Present Publishing)*

The Railway Magazine
Railway World
Trains Illustrated

Right Apart from Snow Hill and New Street, central Birmingham boasted another station – the GWR terminus at Moor Street. This view of the station was taken on 13 November 1985, and shows the 1140 service to Shirley waiting to leave platform 3, and also the empty stock of the 1210 to Stratford-upon-Avon via Henley-in-Arden. A new through station (to Snow Hill), built by the side of the old one, was opened in September 1987, shortly after which the old station was closed, although it survives and there is hope that one day it my become a museum. Moor Street and the North Warwickshire line to Stratford are dealt with in detail in my companion volume *British Railways Past & Present Special: Snow Hill to Cheltenham. RS*

CONTENTS

INTRODUCTION

Like Worcestershire (*British Railways Past & Present No 33*), Warwickshire was affected by boundary changes in the early 1970s with the creation of the West Midlands metropolitan county. However, as in the Worcestershire volume, this one follows the old county boundaries, which, of course, included all of Birmingham and Coventry, as well as the commuter towns of Solihull and Sutton Coldfield.

From the 1920s two railway systems dominated the county of Warwickshire – the Great Western (GWR) and the London Midland & Scottish (LMS) – with the London & North Eastern (LNER) in the shape of the former Great Central main line crossing the eastern fringes at Rugby. Both the GWR and the LMS had main lines from Birmingham to London, as well as many secondary main lines and branches throughout the county. The former London & North Western Railway (LNWR) West Coast Main Line (WCML), later part of the LMS system, runs along the eastern edge of the county from Rugby to Nuneaton and Atherstone, a section popularly known as the Trent Valley Line. Also cutting through the heart of the county is the former Midland Railway Derby-Bristol main line, also later LMS, providing a major link between the North East and the South West/South Coast areas. Add to this the lines to Leicester and East Anglia, Worcester and Hereford, Wolverhampton and Shrewsbury (Cambrian lines), Stafford and Crewe (North Wales and Scotland), plus Manchester and Liverpool, and it is soon realised that Birmingham is the hub of the British railway system.

Warwickshire was a county of contrasts: to the north and north-east of the county there were many coal mines, and even in the northern suburbs of Birmingham there was a mine at Hamstead (just north of Perry Barr), which only closed in the mid-1960s. Today, of course, the motor industry, despite its recent vicissitudes, still dominates the Birmingham and Coventry conurbations, but to the south of these cities there is much splendid countryside, dominated by the historic towns of Stratford-upon-Avon and the county town of Warwick, as well as the Georgian splendours of Leamington Spa. In the south-east of the county is the ancient town of Rugby with its famous public school.

The first railway in Warwickshire was opened in 1838 to provide a link between London and Birmingham; it was built by the London & Birmingham Railway, later to become part of the LNWR. Curzon Street station (part of which is still there today) was the first Birmingham terminus, but this was superseded when New Street station opened in 1854. The GWR opened its line to London in 1852, and within a few years the county was well served by many railway lines, most of which, with the exception of some secondary main lines and branch lines, remain today.

Roger Siviter
Evesham

Opposite Warwickshire contrasts: ex-LMS Class '8F' 2-8-0 No 48492 runs light-engine westwards on the line from Water Orton to Walsall north-east of Birmingham. The location is Sutton Coldfield Park and the date is 10 May 1966. This line closed to passengers in 1965 and is now a freight-only route, starting just west of Water Orton station and used by many of the goods trains that work in and out of Bescot (Walsall) yard. It is also useful as a Birmingham avoiding line, and is popular with enthusiasts' specials. The line's busiest time was in the summer of 1957, when Sutton Park was host to the World Scouting Jamboree, which entailed many special trains.

The second photograph shows winter on Hatton Bank in the south of the county. Class 56 diesel-electric No 56085 heads up the bank with a 'merry-go-round' (MGR) train on the afternoon of 16 February 1983. The location is near Hatton station, where the line parallels the earlier Grand Union Canal. *Both RS*

Map of the railways in central Birmingham

Birmingham New Street

NEW STREET (1): Our journey through the railways of Warwickshire starts at Birmingham New Street station on what was known as the Midland side – platforms 7 to 11 – platforms 1 to 6 being the North Western side. The two sets of platforms, although interconnected at either end of the station, were divided by Station Drive. There was also a pedestrian walkway across the width of the station, which, if my memory serves me correctly, was closed one day a year to maintain it as a private right of way. The first view, taken in the late 1950s, shows an evening rush-hour diesel multiple unit (DMU) about to depart from platform 9 for Castle Bromwich. Just above the rear of the train can be seen the abovementioned pedestrian bridge.

New Street, opened in 1854, was completely rebuilt in the mid-1960s with the advent of the West Coast electrification scheme. The 'present' picture shows the 1506 to Bournemouth (HST unit No 43087) at platform 11A on 29 May 1998. This is roughly equivalent to the 'past' scene, as there are now 12 platforms for passenger use, as opposed to just 10 in the old station, platform 11 being used almost exclusively as a parcels bay – note the parcels lorries on the left-hand side of the older picture, between platforms 10 and 11. Next to bay platform 11 were the back sidings used for fish traffic, Birmingham's fish market being only a short distance away. In my trainspotting days, around 1948-52, I would often see ex-Midland Railway '2Ps' and Compound 4-4-0s lurking around this area. *RS collection/RS*

NEW STREET (2): On Saturday 15 July 1959 ex-LMS 'Patriot' Class 4-6-0 No 45506 *The Royal Pioneer Corps* waits to leave the south-western end of platform 9 with the 12.52pm York to Bristol (Temple Meads) train. These handsome 4-6-0s were first introduced in 1933 (a rebuild of the LNWR 'Claughton' Class), and some were rebuilt in 1946 with a large taper boiler, new cylinders and a double chimney. By 1966 they had all been scrapped, with none alas surviving into preservation.

Today's scene shows DMU No 150210 leaving platform 10 with the 1515 to Worcester and Great Malvern. A comparison with the earlier picture shows some similarities around the bridge area, and also the top of the building in the top left-hand corner. Note in both pictures the tracks leading into the parcels bay.
Michael Mensing/RS

NEW STREET (3): This scene at New Street is facing the other way from the pictures on page 9, and shows ex-Midland Railway Class '4P' 4-4-0 Compound locomotive No 41025 running between platforms 9 and 10 on 6 September 1952. Note the shed code – 22B (Gloucester). In the present-day station on the evening of 24 January 1983 Class 25 diesel-electric No 25123 is seen at platform 9 with a southbound parcels train. *F. W. Shuttleworth/RS*

Bristol main line to Longbridge

FIVE WAYS: After leaving the Midland side of New Street station, we head out on the main line to Bristol, passing through a succession of gloomy tunnels (with for southbound trains a gradient of around 1 in 80). When I left the Army in 1957, one of my first professional music jobs was at the West End Ballroom in Suffolk Street, situated right on the top of the first of these tunnels, and many was the time in the bandroom (which overlooked the line as it came out of the tunnel) when the smoke would drift in through the window! The line then emerged into Five Ways station, and this view (looking towards Bristol) was taken in the 1950s; note the lower-quadrant signals and,

in the top left-hand corner of the picture, the delivery vans belonging to Kunzle, the well-known firm of bakers.

Today's view of Five Ways, taken on 24 May 1998, shows the new station opened in 1978, the old one having closed in 1950, and just two tracks instead of four; the tracks on the left of the 'past' picture led north to the Central Goods Depot.

Lens of Sutton/RS

UNIVERSITY (I): The Bristol line heads south through the Birmingham suburb of Edgbaston, passing the site of the junction for the Central Goods Depot (situated just south of New Street station) and the long-closed stations at Church Road and Somerset Road. For most of the journey, until just south of Bournville, the line parallels the 200-year-old Worcester & Birmingham Canal. On a very wintry 25 January 1984, English Electric Class 50 No 50017 *Royal Oak* heads past the grounds of Birmingham University with the 0735 Plymouth to New Street service. On the left of the picture is the canal, and at the rear of the train is University station, which opened in 1978.

Today's view, taken on 4 May 1998, shows the 'Devon Scot', powered by HST No 43197. This train leaves Plymouth at 0725 and terminates at Aberdeen – a journey of nearly 700 miles. The line has now been electrified as far as Barnt Green and on to the Redditch branch, to give a cross-city service from Lichfield. Considerable building work has taken place in the University grounds. *Both RS*

15

UNIVERSITY (2): By January 1982 all the English Electric 'Deltic' locomotives had been withdrawn from service on BR. However, since the end of August the previous year a series of farewell specials had been run over a wide variety of routes, thus enabling many enthusiasts all over the country to have a final look at these very popular locomotives at work on the main lines. On 28 November 1981 No 55002 *The King's Own Yorkshire Light Infantry* heads through University station with a York-Birmingham-Swindon-Paddington special. Note the headboard, depicting No D9000 *Royal Scots Grey* painted in the original two-tone green livery. First introduced in 1961, happily several 'Deltics' have been preserved, including No 55002.

There is no 'Deltic' in today's picture (although it is still possible, as some of them now run on specials), but instead DMU No 158797 arriving at University station on 4 May 1998, forming the 1030 Nottingham-Cardiff service. The main change over the years has been the electrification, together with some new fencing and lights. *Both RS*

BOURNVILLE (1): After running through Selly Oak station, the line passes through the world-famous Birmingham suburb of Bournville, home of Cadbury's chocolate. This view of the station was taken around the early 1900s from the east side of the line. Beyond the station can be seen the chimneys of the chocolate factory and some of the housing built by the company, one of the first 'garden'-type villages to be built and now part of the Bournville Village Trust. Having lived in the Bournville Village Trust for ten years, I can confirm its village atmosphere, almost unique in such a large city. Also note in the bottom right-hand corner the Worcester & Birmingham Canal.

Today's view, taken on 25 September 1998, shows the factory and canal still prominent, but also a new station with all modern amenities. *Lens of Sutton/RS*

BOURNVILLE (2): On 16 April 1955 ex-LMS Class '5' 4-6-0 No 44842 starts a special train away from just south of Bournville station, having taken over from ex-GWR 'Castle' Class 4-6-0 No 7017 *G. J. Churchward*, which had worked the train up the Lickey Incline, assisted by 0-10-0 No 58100. The 'Black Five' worked the special on to New Street, then on to Bordesley Junction, where 'Castle' Class No 7007 *Great Western* was waiting to relieve the LMS 4-6-0 for the return run to Paddington, from where it had started out. This special, known as 'The Lickey Limited', was organised by *Trains Illustrated*/Ian Allan Ltd, and on the outward journey ran via Didcot and Cheltenham. To the right of the picture can be seen Bournville shed and pathway; the shed was a sub-shed of Saltley, and the roundhouse could accommodate around 25 locomotives. It closed in 1960.

Today's view at roughly the same location shows electric multiple unit (EMU) No 323219 forming the 1301 Redditch to Lichfield service on 25 September 1998. The shed site is now a housing estate. *RS Carpenter collection/RS*

KINGS NORTON (1): One of the popular English Electric Class 40 diesel-electric locomotives, No 40195, approaches Kings Norton with the southbound 'Solent Explorer' to Eastleigh for an open day on 29 May 1983. The Class 40s were first introduced in 1958, but had been withdrawn by the mid-1980s, although some remain in preservation. On the right of the picture is the Camp Hill relief line, used mainly for freight but sometimes for passenger working, notably on summer Saturdays (see the pictures on pages 48-9). The two lines are also connected by the Lifford curve less than a mile north of this junction. The stations on the Camp Hill line closed during the Second World War due to economies, and this became permanent by the end of 1946.

Fifteen years later, on 4 May 1998, we see the rear of EMU No 323209 as it heads north with the 1301 Redditch to Lichfield service. From this location to north of Barnt Green there are four tracks, quadrupling having taken place in 1930 to, among other things, provide relief for holiday traffic. *Both RS*

KINGS NORTON (2): Our next view, taken in the early 1960s, shows ex-LMS Rebuilt 'Royal Scot' Class 4-6-0 No 46137 *The Prince of Wales's Volunteers (South Lancashire)* with a northbound express composed of mixed chocolate-and-cream and maroon stock.

The past picture was taken from the island platform which, as can be seen from the present picture, taken on 25 May 1998, is now closed as EMU No 323208 heads through the station with the 1331 Redditch to Lichfield service. This wider view shows the same footbridge in full, albeit with the entrance blocked to the island platform, and also some of the old station buildings on the left-hand side. The main station building is now situated by the Redditch road bridge, behind the photographer. To the left of the track in the picture are the remains of the carriage sidings, which became a loading area for British Leyland vehicles, then a site for the Cross-City Electrification, which opened between Lichfield and Redditch in the summer of 1993. *Joe Moss/RS*

LONGBRIDGE: The final picture on the Bristol main line was taken just north of Halesowen Junction at Longbridge, just under 7 miles from New Street, in the summer of 1955, and shows ex-LMS Class '5MT' 'Crab' 2-6-0 No 42900 with a northbound fitted freight train. At the rear of the train is Longbridge Lane bridge, and at the extreme upper right-hand corner of the picture can be seen the edge of the massive Austin Motor Company works. The branch line to Halesowen ran westwards through the northern end of the works, where there was a station situated near the Bristol Road (A38) for the convenience of the many Austin workers from both the Birmingham area and the Black Country. Although the line from Halesowen and Old Hill was closed to passengers in the 1920s, the workmen's trains from Old Hill to Longbridge ran until 1958, with the line closing between Longbridge and Halesowen in 1963, and completely in 1969. Details of this line can be found in *British Railways Past & Present, No 33 Worcestershire*.

Today on the site of the 'past' picture there is a station at Longbridge, opened in 1978. On 25 May 1998 DMU No 153857 hurries through with the 1425 Worcester Shrub Hill to New Street (via Bromsgrove) service. Part of the Halesowen Junction line, which now runs just into the present-day Rover works, can be glimpsed under the new Longbridge Lane bridge. *RS Carpenter collection/RS*

North-west Birmingham

BIRMINGHAM NEW STREET: Back at New Street again, this time we are on the North Western side. The date is 20 April 1955, and 'Britannia' 'Pacific' 4-6-2 No 70031 *Byron* has just arrived at platform 3 with the 12.45pm from Manchester London Road. On the left is an unidentified Fairburn or Stanier 2-6-4 tank locomotive with a local train, possibly for Walsall. As on the Midland side of the station, the North Western was also spanned by a fine overall roof, but due to bomb damage in the Second World War it was replaced with individual platform canopies in 1948.

The 'present' picture shows Class 47 diesel-electric No 47840 at platform 2 on 3 July 1999 with the 1040 Edinburgh to Brighton train, which departs at 1602 from New Street. There in hardly anything to compare with the past view except the position of the platforms and what looks like the original brick retaining wall on the right-hand side of the picture. New Street is surmounted by The Pallasades shopping centre, emphasising the fact that the station is slap bang in the city centre. This was brought home to me many years ago when I was chatting to a signalman at Plumpton Junction (near Barrow-in-Furness), who asked me if I could guess where he and his family went for a shopping spree. I replied either Preston or Manchester. 'No,' he said, 'we always go to Birmingham, because as soon as we get out of the train we are right in the shopping centre!' *Brian Moone/RS*

MONUMENT LANE (1): Ex-LMS Fairburn Class '4MT' 2-6-4 tank No 42267 has just left New Street north tunnel with an empty stock train, and is approaching Monument Lane station on the line to Wolverhampton in around 1950-52. On the right-hand side is the edge of Monument Lane locomotive shed (2IE).

On 27 June 1999 we see the rear of DMU No 150127 as it heads for New Street with an evening local train from Kidderminster (1800) going forward to Stratford-upon-Avon. This more distant view shows how the background has changed from dour factories to domination by the National Indoor Arena, the fine convention centre, the magnificent Symphony Hall (in which as a musician I have had the privilege of playing), as well as many new hotels and restaurants. *Joe Moss/RS*

MONUMENT LANE SHED: This view of the depot (looking towards Wolverhampton) was taken around 1959 and shows a good variety of locomotives on shed, including (from right to left) an ex-LMS Class '4F' 0-6-0, Class '3F' 0-6-0 No 43822, 'Black Five' 4-6-0 No 44563, an unidentified 'Jubilee' Class 4-6-0, the rear of a Stanier Class '4MT' 2-6-4 tank, an ex-LNWR Class '7F' 0-8-0, the rear of a 'Black Five' 4-6-0, and finally another unidentified 'Black Five'. Monument Lane shed, together with Aston shed, was responsible for the North Western side of Birmingham, and Saltley and Bournville the Midland lines. *RS Carpenter collection*

MONUMENT LANE (2): LMS Class '4P' 4-4-0 No 1113 runs through Monument Lane station in the early 1930s with an up express. These fine-looking three-cylinder compound locomotives were first introduced by the Midland Railway in 1905, and an example of the class, No 1000, has happily been preserved. On 27 June 1999 only the site of the island platform serves as a reminder of the past. *RS Carpenter collection/RS*

HAGLEY ROAD: A few hundred yards north-west of Monument Lane was the junction for the short branch line to Harborne, some 2 miles south of the Wolverhampton line. This suburban branch opened in 1874, and in its heyday, around 1914, had 27 trains each way, but with stiff competition from buses the passenger traffic declined, and by the end of 1934 it had closed to passengers, although goods traffic continued until the end of 1963. This is Hagley Road station, and in the late 1940s and during the 1950s I would often pass by en route for Birmingham on a Midland Red 130 bus or a Birmingham Corporation Quinton 9 service. From the upper deck – the Hagley Road being right by the station – you got a good view, and often there would be a locomotive shunting in the coal yard at the far end of the platform. From the dress of the passengers, this view of the station, looking from the Hagley Road in the direction of Monument Lane, was taken in Edwardian times. Note the advert for Mulliner Carriages, Mulliner later being one of the coachbuilders for Rolls-Royce cars.

The 'present' view, taken on 3 July 1999, requires no comment... *Lens of Sutton/RS*

ASTON is the next location, 2 miles north of the centre of Birmingham, and also the junction for the line to Bescot (for Walsall) and Wolverhampton to the north-west, and Sutton Coldfield and Lichfield to the north-east, as well as the avoiding line to Stechford on the New Street-Coventry line. On Sunday 15 March 1959 the diverted 4.10pm Wolverhampton (High Level) to Euston train heads south through Aston station for New Street, hauled by ex-LMS 'Jubilee' Class 4-6-0 No 45737 *Atlas*.

Aston station has since been rebuilt, and on 3 July 1999 EMU No 310107 enters the station with the 1400 Walsall to New Street service. *Michael Mensing/RS*

ASTON SHED (21D) was situated south of the station, just beyond the junction of the New Street and Stechford lines. This view, taken on a murky 7 October 1962 from the station end, shows a good variety of locomotives on shed, including 'Britannia' 'Pacifics' Nos 70042 *Lord Roberts* and 70012 *John of Gaunt*, as well as a 'Jubilee' Class 4-6-0, 'Black Five' 4-6-0 No 44342 and other Class '5' 4-6-0s and a Type 2 diesel intruder.

Aston shed was closed in the mid-1960s, and this view, taken from the station on 3 July 1999, shows the Stechford line on the left and the New Street route on the right; between the two is the area once occupied by the shed, which is now used by a coach company. *RS Carpenter collection/RS*

SUTTON COLDFIELD: Heading north-east out of Aston on the Lichfield line, we come to the Royal Borough of Sutton Coldfield. The line to Sutton opened in 1862, but it took another 22 years before the Sutton-Lichfield line was fully opened in 1884. In 1958 Sutton Coldfield became the Midland terminus of a new car sleeper service, first to Stirling, then later to Inverness, Newton Abbot and St Austell; cars would be loaded into the car vans and passengers into the sleeping cars. The service survived until 1972. This view of the station was taken on 7 June 1974, and shows the rear of a three-car WR suburban DMU as it leaves the station as the 5.40pm New Street-Four Oaks service. Out of sight on the left were the sidings used by, among others, the car sleeper service. This area is now a huge commuter car park.

On 27 June 1999 we see the rear of DMU No 150010 as it leaves Sutton with the 1631 Redditch-Lichfield cross-city service, and it would appear that over the years not a great deal has changed. One or two station buildings have gone, and obviously the electric catenary is now in place, but it is still much the same as 25 years earlier.
Michael Mensing/RS

BLAKE STREET: Still on the line to Lichfield, this is Blake Street station, just inside the northern border of Warwickshire, a little over 2 miles north of Sutton Coldfield and 10 miles from New Street. A three-car DMU arrives at the elegant-looking station on 7 March 1973 with the 3.03pm Kidderminster-New Street-Lichfield service.

Unlike Sutton station, Blake Street has been rebuilt, as can be seen from the modern picture, taken on 27 June 1999, of the rear of DMU No 150128 as it leaves the new station with the 1636 Lichfield-Redditch service. *Michael Mensing/RS*

Derby main line to Whitacre

SALTLEY SHED (I): The old Midland Railway shed at Saltley (BR No 21A) was responsible for the Bristol route trains and the Derby and Leicester lines. This large depot, which was situated by the Derby/Leicester lines, consisted of several sheds. Saltley (together with Tyseley) retained an allocation of steam locomotives right up to the end of steam in the Birmingham area, in December 1966. On 15 May 1966 BR Standard Class '9F' 2-10-0s Nos 92151, 92164 and 92104, together with 'Black Five' 4-6-0 No 45349, are grouped around the LMS turntable of No 3 shed, the site of which is now covered by factory units, as seen in the 4 May 1998 photograph. *Both RS*

SALTLEY SHED (2): This scene shows Saltley No 1 shed with BR Standard Class '4MT' 2-6-0 No 76040, two 'Black Fives' and a breakdown crane on 15 May 1966. The site of the old No 1 shed is now used as a diesel depot, and on 4 May 1998 Class 47s Nos 47286 and 47306 were to be seen together with other unidentified Class 47s in the background. For permission to take the 'present' pictures and for information about the depot, I am more than grateful to the friendly and helpful depot staff. *Both RS*

BROMFORD BRIDGE (1), the location for this next series of photographs, is just over a mile east of Saltley on the Derby/Leicester line, where the elevated M6 motorway now runs parallel with the railway. Adjacent to the main line was the Stewarts & Lloyds Ltd Bromford Tube Works, which had its own internal railway, complete with industrial locomotives and exchange sidings with the BR line. On 14 April 1982 Class 08 No 08068 shunts near the tube works, which can be seen clearly together with the works sidings, etc. At the same location on 3 July 1999 it can be seen that the works has since been demolished. *Both RS*

BROMFORD BRIDGE (2): A wider view of the railway at Bromford Bridge shows, in the first picture, English Electric Class 40 No 40057 heading past the sidings with a freightliner train, possibly bound for the East Coast port of Felixstowe on 14 April 1982. On the left is Saltley gasworks, while on the right is the motorway, and in the background the cooling towers of Nechells power station. A few hundred yards east of here was Birmingham racecourse (Bromford Bridge), which, together with the small station built to serve it, was closed in the 1960s with the construction of the M6.

In the second view, dated 29 February 1992, one of the then new Class 60 diesel-electrics, No 60067, is seen at

Bromford Bridge with an eastbound tank train. In the background, approaching quickly, is ex-GWR 'Castle' Class 4-6-0 No 5029 *Nunney Castle*, and the third photograph shows the 'Castle' (with a Didcot to Sheffield special) overtaking the tank train. The gas works is still there, but the cooling towers have gone.

The fourth scene at Bromford Bridge, taken on 3 July 1999, shows considerable changes, with a brand-new road known as the Heartlands Parkway (A47) spanning the main line and crossing the entrance to the sidings, which has been considerably modified to accommodate the new road. The train is an afternoon New Street to Leicester service formed by DMU No 158861. *All RS*

CASTLE BROMWICH: On 5 September 1959 BR Standard Class '9F' 2-10-0 No 92156 approaches Castle Bromwich station with the summer Saturday 12.15pm Scarborough to Kings Norton train. These powerful freight locomotives were quite often used at this time on such summer Saturday duties.

The station was closed in the early 1960s and by 3 May 1992, when No 43008 hurries through with an afternoon Leeds to Plymouth train, only the eastbound platform remains. On the left-hand side is the Castle Vale estate, which in early post-war years was the site of the British Industries Fair (BIF). This was usually held around May, and involved many extra trains calling at Castle Bromwich station. Each day during the fair two special trains from London reversed at New Street, then ran with fresh motive power to Castle Bromwich, and morning trains from the North and East of England would also stop there with passengers for the fair. There was also a shuttle service operating between New Street and Castle Bromwich, usually hauled by ex-Midland Compound 4-4-0s and Ivatt 2-6-0s.

The final picture at Castle Bromwich was taken on 3 July 1999, and shows an afternoon Leicester to New Street train formed of DMU No 158791. The platform is still there, but the buildings on the right-hand side have been replaced. With the closure of the station, the more recent pictures had to be taken from the road overbridge.
Michael Mensing/RS (2)

WATER ORTON (1): Between Castle Bromwich and our next location, Water Orton, is a double junction for the line to Sutton Coldfield and Walsall (see page 6), which allows access to this route for trains from the east or west. At Water Orton itself, some 2 miles from Castle Bromwich, is the junction of the Derby and Leicester routes. This, together with the Sutton/Walsall line, makes this a busy junction for both passenger and freight trains. On 21 May 1966 well-groomed Standard Class '9F' 2-10-0 No 92077 approaches Water Orton station with an RCTS special train ('East Midlander No 9') from Nottingham to Crewe Works via Walsall, Wolverhampton, Stafford, Market Drayton and Madeley, returning via Stockport, Chinley, Millers Dale and Ambergate to Nottingham. In a few hundred yards the special will take the eastward of the two junctions and run north-eastwards to Walsall via the Sutton Park route.

For many years until the late 1980s the Birmingham to Norwich trains were hauled by Class 31 diesel-electrics, and on a sunny 13 June 1987 No 31146 (in Railfreight livery) heads past the old signal box at Water Orton (which by then was used as a tool store) with the 1420 from New Street to Norwich. By now one of the main lines on the right-hand side has been taken out, as has the crossover on the left.

The present-day scene, taken on 26 June 1999, shows DMU No 158845 heading east through Water Orton with a midday New Street to Leicester train. Sadly the old East Junction box/tool store is in the process of being demolished, as are some of the buildings just out of sight on the right-hand side. Happily the station building is still intact, but only one platform face is now used for stopping trains. *All RS*

43

WATER ORTON (2): Turning round from the previous scenes, we see the junction of the Derby and Leicester lines. On 21 May 1966 ex-LMS Class '8F' 2-8-0 No 48247 approaches Water Orton with a heavy westbound coal train from the Leicester coalfields, and is about to pass BR Standard Class '4' 2-6-0 No 76086 as it takes the line to Nuneaton and Leicester. The line to Derby can be seen at the back of the '8F', and on the right-hand side is a goods loop line. Note also the cooling towers of Hams Hall power station, and the ever-present trainspotters on the long wall.

The next picture, taken some 21 years later on 13 June 1987, shows that the junction layout has been considerably modified, with some lines and crossovers having been taken out. By 1987 the 'Peak' Class diesel-electrics were being withdrawn, and the 1010 (Saturdays only) Scarborough to Paignton train, hauled by No 45134, was one of the last passenger workings for this illustrious class, introduced in 1960. Note also a great rarity – no spotters on the wall!

The 'present' scene, taken on 2 June 1999, almost but not quite copies the old view, as Class 60 No 60054 heads for Derby and Peak Forest with RMC empties. Approaching off the Derby line is Class 37 No 37711 with a westbound permanent way train. The track layout is the same as the previous picture, but Hams Hall power station was demolished some years ago. *All RS*

44

WHITACRE JUNCTION: About 4 miles to the east of Water Orton on the Leicester line is Whitacre Junction, and on 5 May 1963 a two-car Metro-Cammell DMU pass through the station forming the 9.35am Leicester (London Road) to Birmingham (New Street) train. At the back of the train can be seen the line that leaves the Birmingham-Derby line at Kingsbury (4 miles north) to form a triangle with the Birmingham-Leicester line. Whitacre was also the junction for the line to Hampton-in-Arden (on the Birmingham-Coventry line – see page 54), but this closed completely in 1952.

Today the station at Whitacre has long gone, but the junction to Kingsbury remains and also the main goods loop. On 26 June 1999 we see the rear of DMU No 158787 as it heads for Leicester with an afternoon train from New Street. *Michael Mensing/RS*

Inner and east Birmingham

ST ANDREWS JUNCTION: We now leave the eastern side of the county and return to inner Birmingham, where at St Andrews Junction on 19 April 1963 ex-LMS '4F' 0-6-0 No 43949 climbs the 1 in 85 past the junction and heads for Kings Norton and the south-west via the Camp Hill avoiding line (see also page 19) with a neat-looking freight train. This junction, situated a mile and a half east of New Street station, is shown in the accompanying map.

In the second photograph the Saturdays-only 1305 York-Plymouth service, headed by English Electric Class 37 No 37422, is seen at St Andrews Junction on 28 August 1993. On summer Saturdays, because of the amount of traffic, it is not uncommon for passenger trains to and from the South West to use the Camp Hill relief line, which on weekdays is mainly used by freight traffic. Note the factory site on the left-hand side, in course of demolition.

The 'present' scene, on 3 July 1999, shows the rear of DMU No 158789 as it heads for New Street with a train probably from Cardiff. A new housing estate has replaced the old factory. The photographs were taken right by the entrance to Birmingham City Football Club's ground at St Andrews. *Michael Mensing/RS (2)*

STECHFORD: Travelling out of central Birmingham on the line to Coventry, after passing through Adderley Park we arrive at Stechford, where just west of the station is the junction for the avoiding line to Aston (see page 28-9). On 2 June 1959 BR Standard Class '4' 2-6-4 tank No 80039 arrives at Stechford station with the 12.42pm Coventry-Birmingham local train. The locomotive was shedded at Bletchley (1E) and this train was a regular working for Bletchley engines. Note the station booking hall and entrance on the overbridge.

On 3 July 1999 EMU No 323212 pauses at the station with the 1204 Coventry-Wolverhampton service. The station has been completely refurbished with a new entrance and booking hall off the picture on the right-hand side, and the addition of a new footbridge, beyond which is the overbridge seen in the previous picture. *Michael Mensing/RS*

MARSTON GREEN: On 18 March 1961 BR Standard Class '5' 4-6-0 No 73004 is about to pass through Marston Green station with the 12.14pm Watford Junction to Birmingham New Street train. No 73004 was one of the first of this class to be built, entering service in June 1951; it was withdrawn in October 1967. Today's picture at Marston Green shows that the station has been extended and that the level crossing is no more. In the bottom right-hand corner can be seen the pathway to the station where the road used to be, while above the train is the pedestrian bridge that has replaced the level crossing. The coal yard is now a bus terminus, and beyond that is a large car park. The station is adjacent to the end of the main runway at Birmingham International Airport, and by simply turning round on the station footbridge, from which I took this picture, I was able to see a variety of aircraft taking off and landing. On 3 July 1999 EMU No 323221 is about to stop at the station with the 1134 Coventry to Wolverhampton local service. *Michael Mensing/RS*

53

Lines around Coventry

HAMPTON-IN-ARDEN is our next location, and on Sunday 15 June 1958 a three-car Metro-Cammell DMU is seen arriving at the neat-looking station with the 2.50pm Birmingham (New Street)-Coventry-Leamington Spa (Avenue) train. On leaving Coventry, the unit will take the line to Leamington via Kenilworth.

Today's a scene shows a refurbished station at Hampton-in-Arden with an up afternoon express to Euston speeding through on 17 June 1999. *Michael Mensing/RS*

COLESHILL: Hampton-in-Arden was the junction for the Midland line to Coleshill and Whitacre Junction (see pages 46-7), which had a separate station at Hampton-in-Arden, situated a few hundred yards to the north of the LNWR station. Coleshill was the only intermediate station, and this view, facing Hampton, was taken on 1 April 1921. The station was renamed Maxstoke in 1923, although passenger services had finished in 1917; the Coleshill name was transferred to Forge Mills, between Water Orton and Whitacre Junction, which subsequently closed in 1968. The Hampton-in-Arden to Whitacre line closed completely in 1952.

The present-day view of the site, taken on 26 June 1999, shows nothing of the previous scene, but further exploration showed the occupation bridge to be still in existence. *RS Carpenter collection/RS*

BERKSWELL: Some 3 miles south-east of Hampton-in-Arden is Berkswell, which was the junction for the former LNWR line to Kenilworth Junction, where it met the Coventry to Warwick and Leamington line. On 13 September 1959 a DMU comprising a pair of two-car Metro-Cammell units is seen arriving at Berkswell with the 4.05pm Rugby to Birmingham New Street service. The line to Kenilworth Junction and Leamington can be seen in the right background, with the main line to Coventry, Rugby and Euston to the left.

The Berkswell to Kenilworth Junction line was closed in 1965 except for a short spur at Berkswell, which was left for the occasional stabling of the Royal Train. This spur line can be seen (although clearly out of use) in this view taken at Berkswell on 17 June 1999. The rear of EMU No 321415 can be seen departing from the station with an evening local service to Coventry. *Michael Mensing/RS*

KENILWORTH: On Sunday 1 October 1961 a three-car Metro-Cammell DMU arrives at Kenilworth station with the 5.35pm Birmingham New Street to Rugby service. Diverted as a result of electrification work to the west of Coventry station, the train, having travelled via the direct line from Berkswell, will now reverse and take the Coventry line to continue its journey to Rugby. Also in the station is a two-car DMU forming the 6.00pm Leamington Spa (Avenue)-Coventry service, which because of the electrification work will not be going through to Birmingham New Street.

The station at Kenilworth is no more, but the line is now used by trains to Leamington and the South Coast that were diverted from the Birmingham-Solihull-Leamington route in order to serve Birmingham International station as well as Coventry. This picture, taken on 17 June 1999, shows most of the station area and yard, now used as a storage depot, with only the church spire serving to identify it with the 'past' scene. *Michael Mensing/RS*

59

SOUTHAM & LONG ITCHINGTON: Today the former LNWR line from Kenilworth runs into the ex-GWR station at Leamington Spa, but in the past the line ran into Leamington Spa (Avenue) station, which was adjacent to and had connections with the GWR station. The LNWR line then ran on to Rugby via Marton Junction, a few miles east of Leamington, where a line diverged south-east to Weedon on the West Coast Main Line, thus creating another route to the industrial Midlands, not only avoiding Rugby but, if necessary, Coventry. It also provided a connection with the ex-GWR Paddington-Birmingham main line at Leamington. Southam & Long Itchington station was located on the Weedon branch, and on 18 January 1958 ex-LMS Class '2MT' 2-6-2 tank No 41228 arrives with the 2.37pm Leamington Spa (Avenue) to Weedon train. The passenger service between Leamington and Weedon was withdrawn in 1958 and that between Leamington and Rugby in 1959. The line between Marton Junction and Leamington closed in 1966, but between Rugby and Marton Junction, and thence to Southam & Long Itchington, tracks survived until the late 1980s to serve the cement works, trains reversing at Marton Junction to gain the Southam line; the route on to Weedon had closed completely by 1963.

The present-day picture, taken on 13 June 1999, shows the site of Southam & Long Itchington station. The cement works is situated just behind the photographer. *Michael Mensing/RS*

BIRDINGBURY was located on the Leamington to Rugby line roughly halfway between the two famous old towns. The date is Saturday 13 June 1959, the last day of the passenger service, and the train, being propelled out of the station by 2-6-2 tank No 41227, is the 4.30pm Leamington Spa (Milverton) to Rugby (Midland), the last one scheduled to call at the station. Note the lady with the flag and all the local people who have obviously turned out to mark the occasion.

Today nothing remains of the tracks, but the station house is now a very handsome private dwelling, and some of the platform remains. *Michael Mensing/RS*

COVENTRY: We leave rural Warwickshire and arrive at the ancient but modern city of Coventry, almost as famous for Lady Godiva as the fine motor cars that it produces. This delightful vintage scene, looking towards Birmingham, was taken on 1 August 1953 and shows ex-Midland Railway Class '2F' No 58306 on station pilot duties. This veteran 0-6-0 was designed by Johnson, and the class was first introduced in 1878.

In the early 1960s, with the onset of electrification, Coventry station was completely rebuilt. On 17 June 1999 we see the rear of a midday service to Wolverhampton as it departs from Coventry, hauled by a Class 92 electric locomotive – a far cry from the Midland 0-6-0! *Brian Moone/RS*

COVENTRY SHED: I suppose it would be fair to say that Coventry, for all its size and the fact that the railway first appeared in 1838 with the opening of the London to Birmingham route, was never a noted railway town. However, it did possess a small locomotive shed (2F), situated just south of the station between the Euston and Leamington lines. This picture of the shed was taken in 1950, and shows ex-Midland Railway Class '2P' 4-4-0 No 41122 receiving attention. The southern end of the station can be seen and also the line to Leamington. The line to Rugby and Euston is out of sight, running at the back of the shed.

The site of Coventry shed on 17 June 1999 is seen in the second view, the area now being partly occupied by the modern power signal box. *H. F. Wheeller collection, courtesy R. S. Carpenter/RS*

FOLESHILL: While the Leamington branch leaves the main Birmingham to Rugby and Euston line to the east of Coventry station, just to the west is the line to the industrial town of Nuneaton, some 10 miles north of the cathedral city. Ex-LNWR Class '7F' 0-8-0 No 49439 is seen trundling along the Nuneaton line with a northbound freight on 24 June 1961. The location is just south of Foleshill station, some 2 miles north of Coventry.

The Nuneaton line was closed to passenger traffic in 1965, but with the growth of areas like the former mining town of Bedworth, passenger services were reinstated in 1987 with not only trains between Coventry and Nuneaton but further afield to Nottingham and Lincoln. On 17 June 1999 the rear of DMU No 156401 is seen at the same location with the 1600 Nuneaton to Coventry service. New factory units have replaced the old, and the trackwork has been considerably modified. There is also a new pedestrian footbridge. *Michael Mensing/RS*

HUMBER ROAD JUNCTION: Just to the north of Foleshill on the Nuneaton line was Three Spires Junction, which connected with Humber Road Junction on the main Coventry to Rugby line, a distance of come 3½ miles. This was known as the Coventry loop line. Built around 1914, it was closed in the 1960s with electrification of the main line, encroaching evidence of which can be seen in this view of ex-LMS Stanier Class '5' 4-6-0 No 44771 passing Humber Road Junction on 9 November 1963 with an up main-line train. The loop line to Three Spires Junction can be seen clearly.

No trace of the junction and loop line can be seen in today's picture, taken on 17 June 1999, as an EMU hurries through with an up afternoon local service. On the right-hand side can be seen Coventry's famous spires, the tallest being that of the old Cathedral, partially destroyed during the Second World War, and now providing a symbol of peace in the modern world. *Michael Mensing/RS*

Rugby

RUGBY MIDLAND (1): Our next location is the important railway town of Rugby, where the Birmingham line meets the Trent Valley section of the West Coast Main Line, and from where there were lines to Leicester (Midland Railway) and Market Harborough (LNWR), as well as that already mentioned to Leamington. All these lines became part of the LMS system and used Rugby Midland station. There was also a locomotive shed at Rugby (2A), situated on the north-eastern side of the Midland station. The LNER had a toe-hold in Warwickshire in the shape of the former Great Central Railway (GCR) Marylebone to Leicester/Nottingham route, which had its own station at Rugby. On 27 June 1959 ex-LMS Class '4' 2-6-4 tank No 42062 is seen at the west end of Rugby Midland station, having just arrived with the 4.50pm from Leicester (London Road). This route closed in the 1960s.

Almost exactly 40 years later the station still retains its vast roof, but with very little glass left. This view of platform 3 was taken on 13 June 1999; on the left is stabled EMU No 310105. Since the 'present' picture was taken most of the roof has been dismantled. *Michael Mensing/RS*

RUGBY MIDLAND (2): On Whit Monday, 26 May 1958, one of Stanier's illustrious 'Coronation' Class 4-6-2 locomotives, No 46241 *City of Edinburgh*, enters Rugby Midland with the down 'Royal Scot'. The girder bridge in the background carried the GCR line from Leicester to Marylebone, Rugby (Central) station being situated about three-quarters of a mile south of the Midland station.

On 13 June 1999 a Euston to Wolverhampton train (1305 ex-Rugby) enters the station headed by No 90015. The GCR line finally closed in 1969, but two spans of the bridge remain in situ. *Michael Mensing/RS*

RUGBY CENTRAL: We leave the former LMS lines at Rugby for a glimpse of the LNER (GCR). On 24 April 1965 Class '5' 4-6-0 No 45215 beads north out of Rugby Central station with the 2.38pm Marylebone to Nottingham (Victoria) train. By September of the following year these through trains had ceased with the closure of the GCR route between Rugby and the south; however, a DMU service ran between Rugby and Nottingham until 3 May 1969.

The 'present' view, taken on 13 June 1999, shows the GCR line now just as a footpath. In the background can still be seen the road bridge that carries the A428 Rugby to Northampton road. The houses on the left also identify with the 'past' view. *Michael Mensing/RS*

HILLMORTON: Two miles south-east of Rugby Midland station the loop line to Northampton leaves the WCML at Hillmorton. This is also where both lines cross the Oxford Canal, one of a series of waterways, including the River Avon, that run through the Rugby area. On 26 May 1958 ex-LMS 'Jubilee' Class 4-6-0 No 45644 *Howe* climbs out of Rugby past Hillmorton signal box with the 12 noon Manchester (London Road) to Euston train. The Northampton loop line runs at a higher level on the right, and in the distance can be seen the Daventry radio masts.

The earlier picture was taken from a footbridge that spanned the four tracks. Today, two of the tracks and the footbridge have gone, so this picture at Hillmorton, taken on 13 June 1999 and showing the rear of a down afternoon express, was taken from track level. Although the trackwork of the Northampton line cannot be seen, the electric catenary is clearly visible. *Michael Mensing/RS*

Trent Valley line through Nuneaton

RUGBY, TRENT VALLEY LINE: From Rugby northwards to Stafford the WCML is also known as the Trent Valley Line, and was originally built to avoid the congested areas of Coventry, Birmingham and Wolverhampton. On 26 June 1960 rebuilt 'Patriot' Class 4-6-0 No 45521 *Rhyl* heads north out of Rugby on the Trent Valley route with the 11.00am Euston to Workington and Carlisle train. These fine-looking locomotives were an Ivatt rebuild of the original Fowler locomotives that had been introduced in 1933. The rebuilt engines were first introduced after the war in 1946, and sadly none have been preserved.

On 13 June 1999 Class 86/2 electric locomotive No 86247 *Abraham Darby* stands in for the 'Patriot' on a down afternoon passenger train. The Class 86s were introduced in 1965, and the 86/2s were a rebuilt version, appearing in 1972. The WCML has lost one of its running tracks, but some of the background buildings above the train remain the same. *Michael Mensing/RS*

73

NUNEATON TRENT VALLEY: Some 15 miles north of Rugby is the industrial town of Nuneaton, situated just inside Warwickshire near its north-eastern border with Leicestershire. This picture of the town's Trent Valley station was taken on 11 March 1961 and shows a two-car Metro-Cammell DMU leaving as the 4.40pm Tamworth (Low Level) to Rugby (Midland) service.

Today's picture of the station, taken on 26 June 1999, shows that apart from the catenary there are many similarities with the earlier scene. The station canopies are still there, as is the footbridge, and only the roofs on the lift towers have been modified, although that out of sight on platform 1 (to the left) still retains its original pyramid roof. Note also that the island platform has been shortened. To complete today's scene, DMU No 153321 is leaving the outer platform with the 1636 service to Lincoln. *Michael Mensing/RS*

NUNEATON SHED: Nuneaton also possessed a locomotive shed, coded 2B and situated in the fork of the West Coast Main Line and the Coventry branch south of the Trent Valley station. This view of the shed, which was home to mainly freight locomotives, was taken on a murky 7 October 1962. On the left can be seen the main Euston line.

The shed was closed in 1966, and today there is nothing to denote that a busy locomotive depot existed at this location. The only point of comparison is the catenary of the WCML, under construction in 1962 and just visible between the bushes and trees on 26 June 1999. *R. L. Carpenter collection/RS*

NUNEATON ABBEY STREET: As well as the WCML, the former Midland line from Birmingham to Leicester and the East of England passed through Nuneaton, and had its own station at Abbey Street, situated to the east of the Trent Valley station. There was a connecting line between the two routes just east of Abbey Street, before the Leicester line crossed over the WCML and joined the LNWR's Nuneaton-Leicester line at South Leicester Junction. Also, just to the north on the WCML was the junction for the Midland & LNWR joint line to Ashby and Burton-on-Trent, which closed in 1971, and which was also connected to the Midland loop line. Ex-LMS Class '4' 2-6-0 No 43046 arrives at Nuneaton Abbey Street on 12 April 1958 with the 2.26pm Ely to Birmingham train.

Abbey Street closed in 1968 and all its trains now use Nuneaton Trent Valley station; the line to Leicester branches off the WCML just south of the station, while the old loop line is still used by goods trains. This is the site of Abbey Street station on 26 June 1999 – the road overbridge can just be seen through the trees. *Michael Mensing/RS*

Opposite ATHERSTONE is a former mining town some 4 miles north of Nuneaton, and as can be seen from this photograph, taken on 23 May 1961, it boasts a very fine LNWR Trent Valley-style station. Standing in the up platform is ex-LMS 'Jubilee' Class 4-6-0 No 45737 *Atlas*, waiting to leave with the 11.45am Liverpool (Lime Street) to Rugby (Midland) semi-fast train, a journey of some 111 miles, probably stopping at most stations en route. Note the fine-looking elevated signal box positioned between the up and down fast lines.

I have deliberately photographed the present-day train early in order to show the magnificently restored station buildings, which are now used as offices. Approaching on the up fast is No 82122 with an afternoon train for Euston on 26 June 1999. *Hugh Ballantyne/RS*

Above BADDESLEY COLLIERY: As stated before, the north-eastern part of Warwickshire was notable for its coalmining, especially in the Nuneaton area. One of its most famous collieries from a railway point of view was that at Baddesley, about 2-3 miles west of Atherstone near the village of Ensor. Only four Garrett locomotives were built for British industrial systems, the last one working at Baddesley Colliery. This 0-4-4-0, named *William Francis*, was built by Beyer Peacock in 1937 as maker's number 6841. It worked at the colliery until 1966, when it was taken out of service and preserved. I visited the colliery on 15 May 1966 hoping to get a picture of the Garrett, but when I arrived I found that it had been taken out of service and was locked away in the colliery locomotive shed, so I was only able to get a view of the famous engine through a side window. However, posing outside the shed was another of Baddesley's locomotives, *Warwickshire*. This inside-cylinder 0-6-0ST was built by Robert Stephenson & Hawthorns in 1953, maker's No 7752. *RS*

Snow Hill to Hatton

SOHO & WINSON GREEN: We now leave the LMS and concentrate on the other major post-Grouping railway company in Warwickshire, the GWR. Unlike the LMS, with several main lines, the GWR had one principal but very busy route, that from Wolverhampton via Birmingham Snow Hill to London Paddington. Here the up 'Cambrian Coast Express', hauled by one of the handsome ex-GWR 'King' Class 4-6-0s, No 6016 *King Edward V*, hurries through Soho & Winson Green station on the north-western borders of Birmingham and Warwickshire on 25 November 1961.

I was unable to copy the 'past' picture from exactly the same location because that would have meant standing in the running lines. However, this is the site of Soho & Winson Green station today. It is now called Soho Benson Road tram station, one of the new stations on the Wolverhampton to Birmingham Snow Hill rapid tramway, which uses the trackbed of the former GWR Snow Hill to Wolverhampton main line. Approaching the new station is tramcar No 13 with an evening Wolverhampton to Birmingham service. On the left are the tracks of the Snow Hill to Stourbridge Junction line, which in a mile or so parts company with the tramway to head south-west to Stourbridge and Worcester. *Michael Mensing/RS*

BIRMINGHAM SNOW HILL (1): When I started trainspotting around 1948, I liked nothing better than to spend the day at Snow Hill station, usually on the end of platform 6, to watch a succession of trains climb the 1 in 47 from Hockley up to the station. These trains were usually hauled by 'Kings', 'Castles', 'Halls', 'Granges' and sometimes the new 'County' Class. Also, according to my Ian Allan 'ABC' book of the time, I 'copped' a few 'Saints' and 'Stars', including 'Star' Class No 4018 with its magnificent nameplate *Knight of the Grand Cross*. In this picture ex-works Class '5' 4-6-0 No 45039 and ex-LMS 'Coronation' 'Pacific' No 46235 *City of Birmingham* climb up from Hockley and approach Snow Hill on 19 May 1966. The occasion was the movement of *City of Birmingham* from Crewe Works to Birmingham for permanent display at the Science Museum.

The old Snow Hill was closed in 1972, but a new station was opened in 1987. (This station and the first part of the Paddington route to Tyseley are dealt with in detail in the companion volume *British Railways Past & Present Special: Snow Hill to Cheltenham*.) In the 'present' picture DMU No 150108 enters the new Snow Hill with a Stourbridge Junction to Shirley train (1645 ex Snow Hill). At the back and to the right of the train can be seen the track of the new tramway system running between Snow Hill and Wolverhampton. Some of the older buildings still remain, with some modifications. *Both RS*

BIRMINGHAM SNOW HILL (2): Ex-LMS '8F' 2-8-0 No 48550 heads through Snow Hill with a down freight on Saturday 30 April 1966. This view gives some idea of the length of the main platforms, which could accommodate two full-length trains, and also shows off the fine-looking roof.

Today's Snow Hill looks very different from the old station, but it has been built on the same site; between the tracks in both pictures can be seen the girders of the under-line bridge that carried the station over Great Charles Street – now the Queensway. On the extreme left of the picture is the new tram route, which terminates at the far end of the station. *Both RS*

TYSELEY: On 16 May 1966 Class '5' 4-6-0 No 44780 heads through Tyseley station with a mixed goods train bound for Banbury. On the extreme left, below the running lines, is the start of the carriage sidings and locomotive shed area.

Nowadays Tyseley shed is a working museum that among its many duties not only supplies steam locomotives for the 'Shakespeare Express' trains from Snow Hill to Stratford-upon-Avon, but also organises the specials. On 15 June 1999 the station nameboard advises that this is where visitors alight for the railway museum as DMU No 150010 runs into the station forming the 1313 Stourbridge Junction to Shirley service. After leaving the station the train will part company with the Paddington route and head south down the North Warwickshire line, which terminates at Stratford-upon-Avon. Comparison with the 'past' picture shows that many things have changed over the ensuing 33 years. The railway buildings have gone, and some of the running lines, as well as the semaphore signals. However, out of sight behind the flowers are still some carriage sidings and, beyond them, the museum. On the other side of the museum is a diesel maintenance depot, mainly responsible for the many DMUs at work in the West Midlands. Note the station nameboard. *Both RS*

I have included this picture to show the very early days of Tyseley railway museum. The occasion is the first Tyseley open day, a few weeks after the end of steam on BR, 29 September 1968. LMS 'Jubilee' Class 4-6-0 No 5593 *Kolhapur* (with GWR 'Castle' Class 4-6-0 No 7029 *Clun Castle* at the rear) is seen on the shuttle service to and from Tyseley South Junction. Also there that day was LNER 'Pacific' *Flying Scotsman*, which had brought in a special train from Doncaster – at the time it was the only steam locomotive allowed to run on BR. As well as No 4472, there were also LMS '8F' No 48773, GWR 0-6-0 No 3205 and 4-6-0 *Cookham Manor*. The event, which was organised jointly by BR, the *Birmingham Post & Mail* and 7029 Clun Castle Ltd attracted over 20,000 visitors. *RS*

TYSELEY SOUTH JUNCTION (I): On the afternoon of 31 January 1966 a three-car DMU set hurries through Tyseley South junction with a Leamington Spa to Snow Hill local train. The North Warwickshire line can be seen below the church, curving away to Stratford-upon-Avon, with the Paddington lines heading behind the junction signal box. At this stage the main line to Paddington was four-track to just south of Lapworth. Note the many semaphore signals and intricate trackwork.

Today's scene, on 15 June 1999, shows DMU No 150015 forming the 1307 Dorridge to Snow Hill threading the junction, and presents a rather sorrier sight. The signal box and semaphore signals have long gone and the trackwork has been considerably modified. The Paddington line is now only double-track, and a lot of sidings have been taken up. Some of the background buildings have gone, including the church, but the familiar row of terraced homes on the left still remain. *Both RS*

TYSELEY SOUTH JUNCTION (2): Ex-SR 'Merchant Navy' Class 'Pacific' No 35028 *Clan Line* takes the Stratford-upon-Avon (North Warwickshire) line at Tyseley South junction with the 'Thames-Avon Express' special from London on Saturday 2 March 1985. This view clearly shows the booking hall at Tyseley station, which is conveniently situated adjacent to the roadway. Many of the suburban stations on the GWR were of this design.

On 8 January 1997 DMU No 150128 heads down the North Warwickshire line with the 1312 Stourbridge Junction to Shirley service. As stated before, the North Warwickshire line to Stratford-upon-Avon is dealt with extensively in *British Railways Past & Present Special: Snow Hill to Cheltenham*. *Both RS*

ACOCKS GREEN or – as it was originally known – Acocks Green & South Yardley is the first station after Tyseley on the line to Paddington, just 4 miles from Snow Hill. On 4 July 1959 ex-GWR 'King' Class 4-6-0 No 6017 *King Edward IV* makes a splendid sight as it speeds through the old station on the down main line with the 11.10am Paddington to Birkenhead (Woodside) train. The 'King' will come off at Wolverhampton (Low Level) and probably be replaced by a 'Castle' off Wolverhampton Stafford Road shed for the remaining 87 miles to Birkenhead.

Nowadays there are only two tracks through Acocks Green and one island platform, and a car park occupies the area where the relief tracks were. Bushes and trees obscure a Class 150 unit as it pauses at the station with the 1423 Dorridge to Stourbridge Junction service on 15 June 1999. *Michael Mensing/RS*

SOLIHULL: After Acocks Green the line runs through Olton and arrives at the commuter town of Solihull. This view of Solihull station and goods yard was taken on 10 August 1957, and shows ex-GWR Class '4300' 2-6-0 No 6379 heading for Birmingham Snow Hill with the 8.50am from Margate.

A comparison with today's picture, taken on 15 June 1999 and showing No 150127 forming the 1507 Dorridge to Snow Hill service, illustrates the decline of the railway system in this area over the years. There is no longer a goods yard, and just two tracks with one island platform for the station. However, on a more positive note there is now an hourly service from Snow Hill to London Marylebone and return via Banbury, which is proving popular and attracting passengers back to the route. *Michael Mensing/RS*

BENTLEY HEATH CROSSING: After leaving Solihull the Paddington line heads south-eastwards through the pleasant Warwickshire countryside, passing first Widney Manor station then Bentley Heath Crossing, where these next pictures were taken. It is 8.20am on the morning of the glorious 1 June 1966, and an unidentified BR Standard Class '9F' 2-10-0 is approaching the crossing with an up coal train, probably heading for Didcot and its power station.

Except for the level crossing area, today's scene is quite difficult to identify with the 'past' picture, as DMU No 150018 heads towards Birmingham as the 1522 Leamington Spa-Great Malvern service on 15 June 1999. *Both RS*

KNOWLE & DORRIDGE is some 10 miles south-east of Snow Hill, and the station serves the attractive commuter area that has grown over the years with the prosperity of Birmingham and its industries. Ex-GWR 'Castle' Class 4-6-0 No 7008 *Swansea Castle* waits to leave the station on Sunday 10 July 1960 with the 4.05pm Wolverhampton (Low Level) to Oxford slow train. On the right is the 4.30pm Wolverhampton to Paddington service, with which the Oxford train connects.

The station is now known simply as Dorridge, but apart from the loss of the left-hand platform many features remain from the earlier picture, notably the station buildings on the main up platform and part of the old GWR footbridge, which still looks in good order. Waiting to leave the side platform is No 150019 with the 1606 service to Snow Hill, while on the up platform some passengers are already waiting for the next train, the 1630 Snow Hill to Marylebone service, which is not due into Dorridge until 1649, and arrives at the London terminus at 1846. *Michael Mensing/RS*

LAPWORTH (1): It is around 8.30am on 2 June 1966 as ex-LMS Class '5' 4-6-0 No 44661 heads down the four-track section between Dorridge and Lapworth with a south-bound parcels train bound for Leamington Spa and Banbury. From the same spot almost exactly 33 years later, on 1 June 1999, all that can be seen are bushes and trees. *Both RS*

LAPWORTH (2): Moving to the road bridge (the second overbridge north of Lapworth), just a few yards from where the previous pictures were taken, we see English Electric Class 50 No 50034 *Furious* on 16 February 1983 heading for Leamington Spa with the empty coaches of a VSO Pullman train, which had earlier worked into Leamington from Paddington, the stock being stored at Tyseley prior to the return to Paddington. Note that the main line is now only two-track, and also the new livery on the locomotive, which had just been introduced with their refurbishment, although some retained the old livery even after refurbishment, as seen opposite.

On 1 June 1999 'Turbo' unit No 165036 is seen at the same location with the 1330 Birmingham Snow Hill to Marylebone service. The undergrowth is gradually taking over the old trackbed. *Both RS*

LAPWORTH (3): Turning round from the scenes opposite, we see Class 50 No 50030 *Repulse* (still in the old livery) with a midday Paddington to Birmingham (New Street) train, also on 16 February 1983. The Class 50s took over on this route when the 'Western' Class diesel-hydraulics were withdrawn in 1977, and carried on working until 1989, by which time the 50s themselves had started to be withdrawn. As several have been preserved, a member of this popular Class might occasionally be seen on this route on special charters.

Nowadays, the only regular loco-hauled trains to the Birmingham area via Hatton (the inter-city services to the South Coast run via Coventry and Kenilworth) are freights, and even these are few on the ground. Here Class 47 No 47286 is seen heading for Birmingham with a heavy freight on I June 1999. *Both RS*

LAPWORTH (4): After steam traction finished on BR on 11 August 1968 there was a ban on the use of steam locomotives on BR, with one exception – LNER 'Pacific' No 4472 *Flying Scotsman*, then owned by Mr Alan Pegler. On 29 September 1968 (on the occasion of the Tyseley open day already seen on page 85) No 4472 had worked to Birmingham with a special train from Doncaster, then ran a special from Tyseley to Leamington Spa. The train is seen just north of Lapworth on its way to Leamington.

'Sprinter' unit No 158748 is seen at the same location on 1 June 1999 forming the 1211 Worcester Shrub Hill to Leamington Spa service. The four-track section between Tyseley and Lapworth was reduced to two tracks around 1970. *Both RS*

LAPWORTH (5): Lapworth station, about 12 miles from Snow Hill, was where the four tracks finished. Approaching the station on the up main line is ex-SR 'Merchant Navy' 'Pacific' locomotive No 35026 *Lamport & Holt Line* with the return leg of 'The Aberdonian' railtour on Sunday 26 June 1966. This very ambitious tour, which was organised by the Warwickshire Railway Society, started out from Waterloo at 10.30pm on Friday 24 June, and covered the following itinerary: Waterloo, Banbury, Birmingham, Market Drayton, Crewe, Manchester, Hellifield, Carlisle, Hawick, Edinburgh, Larbert, Alloa, Thornton, Dundee, Aberdeen, Forfar, Perth, Edinburgh, Doncaster, Nottingham, Dudley, Old Hill, Birmingham, Banbury, and back to Waterloo. A variety of locomotives were used on the special train (which included sleeping cars and a restaurant car) – apart from No 35026, there was ex-LMS 'Jubilee' 4-6-0 No 45581 *Bihar and Orissa*, LNER 'Pacific' No 4472 *Flying Scotsman*, ex-LNER 'J37' 0-6-0s Nos 64570 and 64618, ex-LNER 'A4' 'Pacific' No 60024 *Kingfisher*, BR Standard '9F' 2-10-0 No 92113, as well as an ex-LNER Class 'V2' 2-6-2 and an ex-LMS Class '5MT' 2-6-0. When I took this picture at Lapworth it was late afternoon, so it would be at least early evening before arrival at Waterloo – some special! The picture also shows the neat layout at Lapworth, complete with semaphore signals.

The view from the same location on 1 June 1999 is of a storage yard and the back gardens of new homes where there used to be railway track. The two tracks now remaining are out of sight behind the bushes. *Both RS*

HATTON (1): After leaving Lapworth the line passes through Rowington (where Lapworth water troughs were situated) then runs through Hatton North and East Junctions (for Stratford-upon-Avon) before entering Hatton station. On 6 August 1962 ex-GWR 'Castle' Class 4-6-0 No 4096 *Highclere Castle* passes through the station with a southbound express. At the rear of the train can be seen Hatton East Junction, which with the North Junction forms a convenient triangle, ideal today for turning the steam locomotives that work the special charter trains to Stratford.

Today Hatton station is still in good order, with new waiting rooms. On 1 June 1999 DMU No 150216 enters the station with the 1055 Great Malvern to Leamington Spa service. The line from Stratford now only enters the station by the side of the island platform. Note also that there is a connection from this line to the main line to Birmingham, thus forming a loop line if required. *Brian Moone/RS*

BEARLEY: We leave the main line at Hatton to take a trip on the branch to Stratford-upon-Avon. This location is Bearley, and we are looking south towards Stratford. At the end of the platforms on the right-hand side is East Junction, this line leading to North Junction, on the North Warwickshire line. The line to Alcester also ran from North Junction, thus providing a through route from the GWR's Paddington main line to the LMS Redditch/Ashchurch line. However, the line to Alcester closed in 1951.

There is very little of the past left at Bearley on 1 June 1999 – just one platform and the remains of the other. However, the station house (off the picture to the right) is nicely preserved and in private hands. *Lens of Sutton/RS*

HATTON (2): We rejoin the main Birmingham to Paddington line at Hatton station on 23 September 1957, as one of the ex-GWR 'King' Class locomotives, No 6024 *King Edward I*, enters the station with the 9.10am Paddington to Birkenhead (Woodside) train. Happy to say, this handsome engine has been preserved. It was rescued from Barry scrapyard by the 6024 Preservation Society, restored at Quainton Road, and is now a regular performer on the main line; in the last couple of years I have seen it at work from Cornwall in the South West to Ais Gill on the Settle & Carlisle route, and of course from time to time it works the Paddington to Birmingham route. Note on the right-hand side the track running into the side platform for local trains to Stratford.

Colour lights have replaced the semaphore signals as DMU No 150129 runs into Hatton with the 1222 Leamington Spa to Great Malvern service on I June 1999. One or two sidings have now gone, but the line to Stratford is still in place and well used, with a regular service to and from Leamington Spa. *Michael Mensing/RS*

HATTON BANK: On 26 July 1966 '8F' 2-8-0 No 48477 climbs the 1 in 110 up Hatton bank with a Banbury-Birmingham goods train. This location is about a mile east of Hatton station, where the line runs near to the Grand Union Canal.

These days its is rare to see a locomotive-hauled passenger train on Hatton bank. However, from time to time special charter trains can be seen, as on 16 August 1997 when Class 56 No 56055 was photographed heading down the bank with a return special charter train from Stratford-upon-Avon to Reading organised by Hertfordshire Railtours. *Both RS*

Through Warwick and Leamington

WARWICK: Although the historic county town of Warwick boasts the finest mediaeval castle in England and perhaps Great Britain, unlike its near neighbour Leamington Spa it was never regarded as an important railway centre. The Coventry-Kenilworth-Leamington line skirts its eastern boundary (there was a station at Milverton), but running through the heart of the town is the Birmingham-Paddington line, with Warwick station itself just off and above the A46 Coventry road, and very near to the town centre. Seen here in the early 1950s, ex-GWR Class '4300' 2-6-0 No 6363 heads through Warwick with a northbound freight. The small goods yard, which closed many years ago, was situated behind the photographer, off the down line.

On I June 1999 Class 47 No 47376 with a northbound freightliner train re-enacts the past scene. A comparison shows that the station has been considerably rebuilt, and the bay platform taken out to accommodate more car parking. *R. S. Carpenter collection/RS*

LEAMINGTON SPA (1): The Georgian spa town of Leamington is a busy railway town, which was in the past, and is today, a stopping place for all the main passenger trains. Many readers will no doubt remember, as I well do, seeing the Leamington Spa name on some of the carriage nameboards of the Paddington-Wolverhampton trains. Here the up 'Cambrian Coast Express' (perhaps the most famous train on this route) is seen arriving at Leamington Spa (General) with ex-GWR 'King' Class 4-6-0 No 6009 *King Charles II* in charge on 21 May 1960. The station was known as 'General' in those days because almost adjacent on the up side was Leamington Spa (Avenue) station, which served the LNWR Coventry-Leamington-Rugby line (see pages 58-61) and also connected with the Paddington line at the eastern end of the station. The line from Leamington Spa (Avenue) to Marton Junction (for Rugby) was closed in 1966, but the Coventry-Leamington section is used today by inter-city trains to and from the South Coast to the North of England via Birmingham New Street, the junction now being at the western end of Leamington station.

On 13 June 1999 'Turbo' unit No 165014 arrives at Leamington Spa with the 1630 Birmingham (Snow Hill) to Marylebone service. The semaphore signals have gone and some trackwork has been modified, but the platform canopies are still there, as are some station buildings. *Michael Mensing/RS*

LEAMINGTON SPA (2): On Sunday 8 September 1957 ex-GWR 2-6-0 No 5390 trundles through Leamington Spa (General) station with a down iron-ore train. Glimpsed at the rear of the up platform is the former LNWR Coventry to Rugby line through Avenue station. Leamington also had a four-road locomotive shed (84D), which was situated at the south of General station, between the GWR main line and the LNWR line to Rugby, part of which can be seen on the extreme right-hand side at the rear of the iron-ore train. It closed in 1965.

An HST, with power car No 43091 leading and 43068 at the rear, enters Leamington Spa station with the 1657 to Liverpool (Lime Street) on Sunday 13 June 1999. A siding still remains as a reminder of the line to Rugby.
Michael Mensing/RS

HARBURY TUNNEL: After leaving Leamington Spa, the GWR main line to Paddington climbs more or less all the way to the Warwickshire/Oxfordshire border just south of Fenny Compton. The steepest part of this section is the 1 in 143 through Harbury cutting, just north of Harbury Tunnel. On 10 October 1981 unrebuilt English Electric Class 50 No 50028 *Tiger* kicks up a racket as it climbs the steep grade up to the tunnel with a morning Birmingham to Paddington train.

Sixteen years later, in brilliant autumn sunshine on 9 September 1997, Class 47 No 47818 climbs through Harbury cutting with the 0917 Manchester (Piccadilly) to Paddington train.

Opposite are two views from steam days of BR Standard '9F' 2-10-0s at work near Harbury Tunnel on 18 July 1966. In the first No 92090 approaches the southern end of the tunnel with a down mineral train, while in the second No 92219 bursts out of the tunnel with a mid-morning southbound ore train. *All RS*

SOUTHAM ROAD & HARBURY lay about a mile south-east of Harbury Tunnel, where, during the summer of 1936, one of the GWR's illustrious 'Saint' Class 4-6-0s, No 2924 *Saint Helena* is seen with an up van train. This locomotive, designed by Dean and then Churchward, was built in 1907 and scrapped in 1950.

The main line services between Wolverhampton and Paddington remained in the hands of steam power until the winter timetable of 1962, when the Type 4 'Western' Class diesel-hydraulics took over. In the second picture No 1048 *Western Lady* hurries past the site of Southam Road & Harbury station on 17 April 1976 with a Birmingham to Paddington train. The reign of the 'Westerns' was to last until early 1977, by which time the Class was withdrawn. However, unlike the station, of which virtually nothing is now left, happily No 1048 has been preserved at The Railway Age, Crewe.

We complete this trio of pictures with 'Turbo' unit No 165038 running past the station site with the 1030 Birmingham (Snow Hill) to Marylebone service on Sunday 13 June 1999. *R. S. Carpenter collection/RS (2)*

FENNY COMPTON is our final location on the GWR main line in Warwickshire. Some 9 miles north of Banbury, it was also the junction for the Stratford-upon-Avon & Midland Junction Railway (SMJ), which ran due west from Ravenstone Wood Junction on the MR Northampton to Bedford line across to Broom Junction on the Redditch/Ashchurch line, also formerly Midland Railway. Although the SMJ line closed to passenger traffic in 1952, it was always a popular route for specials, right until its closure in 1965. One such railtour ran on 24 April 1955 between Banbury and Stratford-upon-Avon, hauled by ex-GWR Class '9000' 4-4-0 No 9015. The special is seen here standing on the SMJ side of Fenny Compton station.

The present-day view of Fenny Compton station was taken on Saturday 29 May 1999 with a midday northbound inter-city service. The old signal box has long gone, but the edge of the new one can be seen, and on the right-hand side there remains some of the old platform. Note also the SMJ lines still in place, for although the line closed in 1965 a short section to just east of Kineton was retained for MOD traffic, but nowadays this sees little traffic.

Hugh Ballantyne/RS

Lines around Stratford-upon-Avon

KINETON: After Fenny Compton the next station westwards along the Stratford-upon-Avon & Midland Junction line was Kineton, and here we see the 'South Midlander' special of 24 April 1955 headed by No 9015 as it pauses for a photographic stop on its outward journey. The charter train was organised by the Railway Enthusiasts Club.

Today the site of Kineton station is mainly a car park for an industrial plant. The road overbridge in the 'past' picture is obscured by trees in this 29 May 1999 photograph. *Hugh Ballantyne/RS*

STRATFORD-UPON-AVON OLD TOWN: The same railtour is now seen at Stratford-upon-Avon's SMJ station at Old Town, taking water prior to returning to Banbury via Broom Junction, Honeybourne and Moreton-in-Marsh, from where there was an additional trip to Shipston-on-Stour (see overleaf). Note on the right-hand side the locomotive shed.

The SMJ line closed in 1965, and today at the site of Old Town station all that there is to remind us of the past is a walkway on the old trackbed, and a buffer stop hidden amongst the bushes behind the photographer.
Hugh Ballantyne/RS

SHIPSTON-ON-STOUR provides our final view of the 'South Midlander' special, the train having been hauled from Moreton-in-Marsh by GWR 'Dean Goods' 0-6-0 No 2474. In a short while the locomotive will run round its train for the return journey to Moreton. This was the last trip for this veteran locomotive before withdrawal, but No 2516 of this famous Class, introduced in 1883, is preserved at Swindon Railway Museum.

The Shipston branch had been closed to passengers since 1929, and was closed completely by the early/mid-1960s. This is the view of the station site on 24 May 1999, which still contains the goods building and trackbed. However, on that day I was reliably informed locally that the site was about to be turned into a housing estate! *Hugh Ballantyne/RS*

BROOM JUNCTION (1): About 6 miles west of Stratford-upon-Avon was Broom Junction, where the SMJ line connected with the MR Barnt Green/Redditch line to Evesham and Ashchurch, otherwise known as the Birmingham to Gloucester loop line. This first view was taken around 1930 and is looking south towards Ashchurch, with the SMJ line from Stratford coming in from the left-hand side beyond the bridge. Passenger services finished in 1962, with the withdrawal of Redditch to Evesham trains, and the station closed in 1963.

This is the site of Broom Junction today, with some of the trackbed and platform left, and also the background road to identify the location on 31 May 1999. *Lens of Sutton/Christina Siviter*

BROOM JUNCTION (2): This is the view at Broom Junction looking from the road bridge towards Redditch, probably also around 1930. The island platform can be clearly seen, and also the small goods yard. Note also the Midland Railway lower-quadrant signals. With the exception of the background hills, today's picture, taken on 31 May 1999, shows very little to identify it with the earlier scene. *Lens of Sutton/RS*

STUDLEY & ASTWOOD BANK station was on the Barnt Green to Evesham line between Redditch and Alcester; at the latter place there was a connection to the North Warwickshire line, which closed in 1951. On 12 August 1956 a pair of three-car Derby lightweight DMUs passes slowly through with a Birmingham New Street to Evesham Sunday excursion.

The station closed in 1963, and 36 years later on 31 May 1999 only the station house, which is now in private use, can be glimpsed on the left through the foliage. *Michael Mensing/RS*

Special trains in Warwickshire

On the evening of 6 August 1978 GWR 'Castle' Class 4-6-0 No 7029 *Clun Castle* is seen heading towards Kings Norton on the Camp Hill avoiding line near Bordesley with a Tyseley-Hereford train. *RS*

GWR 'King' Class 4-6-0 No 6024 *King Edward I* hurries through Bromford Bridge on 17 March 1991 with a special charter from Didcot to Derby. This was one of the first outings for this handsome locomotive on its return to main-line duty. *RS*

So far, to the best of my knowledge, there has not been any steam working in the rebuilt Birmingham New Street station. However, over the years there have been many diesel specials, including this one on 31 May 1987, when the renowned Pathfinder Tours organised a special train from Bristol to Barmouth and return, seen leaving New Street's platform 7 on the outward journey. It is hauled by a pair of English Electric Class 37s, Nos 37159 and 37204. *RS*

A popular route for steam specials is the North Warwickshire line to Stratford-upon-Avon, which now sees steam charters on a regular basis, the trains appropriately being named 'The Shakespeare Express'. On 5 June 1986 No 7029 climbs out of Woodend and heads for Tyseley with a morning train from Stratford. *RS*

On 12 June 1988 ex-SR unrebuilt 'West Country' 'Pacific' No 34092 *City of Wells* climbs up to Harbury Tunnel with a return Stratford to Marylebone special charter. *RS*

The unique BR Standard Class '8P' 'Pacific' No 71000 *Duke of Gloucester* charges up Hatton Bank with a Didcot to Derby train on 7 April 1990. *RS*

On a beautiful 9 November 1991 GWR 'Castle' Class 4-6-0 No 5029 *Nunney Castle* was photographed near the foot of Hatton Bank with a Paddington-Stratford train. *RS*

INDEX OF LOCATIONS